ADVENTURE WEST
BANFF AND JASPER NATIONAL PARKS

Photography
Hälle Flygare

Text
Elke Emshoff

🄝 **Methuen**

Toronto   New York   London   Sydney   Auckland

PRODUCED BY JÜRGEN F. BODEN
Book design: Hartmut Brückner

PHOTO CREDITS

Hälle Flygare
except

Edi Klopfenstein:	pages 15, 28 (skiing), 41, 43, 49, 54/55, 59 (Jasper), 60, 62, 63, and front cover
Elke Emshoff :	pages 39, 42, 45, 56, 59 (Jasper Park Lodge)
Brian Milne :	pages 14, 52, 61 (coyote)
Valerie J. May :	pages 44, 53
Peter D'Angelo :	pages 5, 6 (train)
Phil Hersee :	pages 21, 29
Peter Clarey :	page 51
A. E. Johann :	rear cover
W. Jack Schick :	page 23

Front cover: Maligne Lake
Rear cover: Mount Robson

ACKNOWLEDGEMENTS

We wish to express our gratitude and appreciation to Parks Canada as well as to Travel Alberta for granting permission to utilize their publications and to reproduce their maps in this book; special thanks are extended to the Superintendents of Banff and Jasper National Parks and to their staff for reviewing all text matter.

Travel Alberta
10065 Jasper Avenue
Edmonton, Alberta
Canada T5J OH4

Travel Alberta
1, Mount Street
Berkley Square
London W1, England

Published in Canada by Methuen Publications, 2330 Midland Avenue, Agincourt, Ontario M1S 1P7

©1983 by Jürgen F. Boden

ISBN 0–458–96320–8

Lithographed, printed and bound in the Federal Republic of Germany by Westermann Druck GmbH, Braunschweig.

INTRODUCTION

"The national parks are part of Canada's natural heritage and should be maintained as a trust so that Canadians – and their visitors – now and in the future can experience undisturbed landscapes of exceptional and distinctive quality – their forms, plants, and wildlife – existing in as nearly a natural state as possible." This is the guideline of the present policy of Parks Canada, who are administering and maintaining all national parks under federal authority, a policy which has not changed much since the proclamation of the National Parks Act in 1930. At first glance, the ideas of use and of preservation may seem to contradict themselves, but this does not necessarily have to be the case. Until the 1960s, the number of people who visited the national parks was relatively small, so the impact on the environment of these wilderness preserves was minimal. In recent years, however, the number of visitors, including an increasing proportion from abroad, has skyrocketed due to increased leisure time and the impact of automobile travel. If the natural heritage of the parks is to be preserved for the future generations, we must learn to care for and respect them.

Unfortunately, the environment of a national park does not have an unlimited potential for use. There may come a time when a park is fill, and no more visitors can be allowed to enter without seriously damaging the natural beauty. It is true that "parks are for people," but only for those who realize that the delicacy of the wilderness can easily be impaired by the wrong behaviour. We must learn to recognize the national park as a very special place to visit – rather than merely a recreation area – having been set aside for us and for the generations to come. It is indeed a privilege to visit any national park, and the general wild quality must be respected at all times. With intelligent and thoughtful use, Canada's national parks can continue as a source of awesome beauty and inspiration.

Banff Springs Hotel, originally built in 1888.

Banff, centre of Banff National Park, with towering Cascade Mountain (2,998 m).

5

The daring sport of hang gliding, as seen here over the Banff area with Mount Rundle (2,999 m) in the background, is no longer permitted within the parks boundaries.

Banff's railway station with a VIA RAIL transcontinental train on CPR tracks, which cross the Canadian Rockies on the southern route.

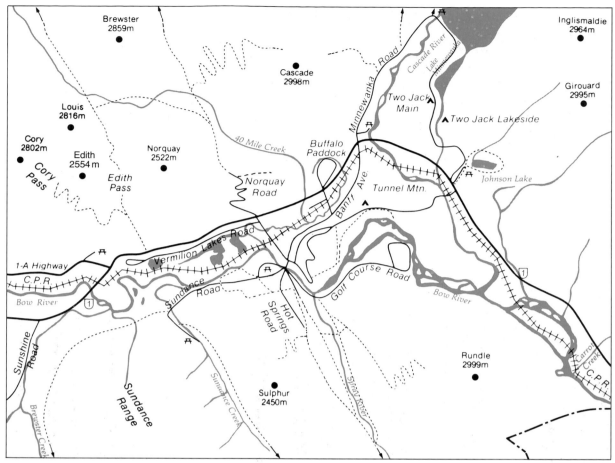

Banff and area.

Here are some basic rules which should be followed by every visitor of a national park.

SAFETY is your own personal responsibility. Travel in wilderness areas can be hazardous. Proper clothing and footwear are survival "musts." The animals in the parks may appear tame, but they are wild and some can be dangerous. Do not feed, approach or harass any animal. Respect their wild and free nature – observe them but do not intrude.

CAMPING is limited to designated areas only on a first-come, first-serve basis. A daily fee is charged with a maximum allowable stay of two weeks unless otherwise posted. If a campground is full, park personnel and signs will direct you to an overflow camping area. Although the Banff and Jasper National Parks are open all year, some facilities and services are available only in summer. Campgrounds in the mountain national parks are open from mid-May to mid-October and limited facilities for winter camping are available during the rest of the year.

WILDERNESS TRAVEL should always be done with a companion; he or she could save your life.
BACKCOUNTRY ACTIVITIES such as hiking and cross-country skiing involving an overnight stay require a park-use permit before each trip. This permit is available free of charge at information centres and warden stations. The permits were introduced to help prevent an overuse of the trails and wilderness areas. If the quota on a particular trail has been reached, park staff will suggest other less crowded areas. Permits are not needed for single day trips.

RISK ACTIVITIES such as mountain hiking, which may be hazardous, are permitted but participants are encouraged to register their travel plans with the park staff at warden stations or headquarters or information centres available in Banff and Jasper National Parks at Banff, Lake Louise, Jasper and elsewhere. If you do register at the commencement of your trip, you must also register on completion of your trip, either in person or by telephoning. If a party is overdue, their registration will alert park staff to the possibility that emergency help may be needed.

CAMPFIRES may only be lit in fireplaces provided in campgrounds, picnic areas and alongside of the trails, or outdoor stoves may be used. Barbecues may be used only in campgrounds and picnic areas. Although

7

Wapiti (elk) bulls in the deep snow of Bow Valley.

fireplaces are located at many backcountry campsites as well, firewood is often scarce and should be used sparingly; campers may not cut their own. Backcountry users are therefore encouraged to carry gas-burning stoves.

LITTER and refuse must be packed and taken out with you from trails and campsites where no garbage disposal facilities exist. Free litter bags are available at registration outlets.

BOATING in rowboats, canoes and kayaks is allowed in most of the lakes and rivers of Banff and Jasper National Parks; in Banff Park, power boats may be used only on Lake Minnewanka; in Jasper Park, power boats may be used only on Lakes Pyramid and Medicine. Boats with electric motors without on-board generators are allowed on any lake where boating is permitted.

MOTOR VEHICLES including automobiles, trucks, motor bikes and all-terrain vehicles are restricted to use on public roads only.

OVERSNOW VEHICLES may be used on designated trails only. Snowmobilers must obtain permits which are available at either the trail heads at permit stations, or at the wardens' offices, or at information centres.

FISHING is allowed in most park waters, and is best in waters not clouded by glacial silt. Anglers must obtain a national park's fishing permit at the information centres or sporting goods stores in the parks, and they must obey the parks' fishing regulations included with permits.

HUNTING is not allowed in national parks.

FIREARMS must be dismantled, or, if not possible, kept in a closed case or be wrapped, in a manner so as not to expose any part of the firearm to view.

PETS should be leashed at all times in national parks.

Our obligation as visitors is to leave the wilderness unimpaired. All wildlife, vegetation and minerals in the parks are protected by law. As visitors, a slogan to remember is, "Take nothing but pictures and your memories; leave nothing but footprints."

Banff Parkwarden Service cabin, closed for the winter, located at Bryant Creek in the southernmost part of the park.

HOW TO GET TO BANFF AND JASPER

Calgary, Edmonton, and Vancouver International Airports serve as gateways to Banff and Jasper National Parks, the largest among Canada's seven mountain national parks, and the most spectacular.

With direct and connecting flights serving all international origins, these airports can accommodate travellers from around the world.

From Calgary International Airport, it is 130 km (81 miles) by road on the westbound Trans-Canada Highway (No. 1) to Banff through the foothills of the Canadian Rockies. All major rental car companies are represented at Calgary's airport. There is a direct Brewster Airporter bus service to Banff available. Shuttle buses from the airport to Calgary connect with a regular Greyhound bus service. At the train terminal, you can board Via Rail's train service to Banff on the CP tracks.

An arrival at Edmonton International Airport provides the visitor with the opportunity to visit Jasper National Park first; the driving distance to Jasper is 384 km (239 miles) on Highway 16 westbound. At Edmonton's airport all major rental car companies are available for service, as well as bus and train (CN) connections.

Vancouver, B. C., arrivals can consider an unforgettable trip to the Canadian Rockies by car, bus, train and through numerous tour packages. The distance to Banff by road is 916 km (569 miles) on the scenic Trans-Canada Highway (No. 1) eastbound. Alternate routes to the Rocky Mountains are the Crowsnest Highway (No. 3), a southern route, and the Yellowhead Highway (Nos. 5 and 16) through British Columbia's interior.

Those wishing to arrive by private plane can make use of the facilities of Springbank Airport located approximately 112 km (70 miles) east of Banff. A 792-metre (2,600 feet) grass airstrip of the Jasper-Hinton airport is located just outside the east park gate and 68 km (42 miles) from the Jasper townsite.

Parks Canada's annual permit of $ 10 is valid in all national parks; the $ 2 four-day permit expires at midnight of the fourth day and a $ 1 permit is valid only on the day of issue. All permits allow unlimited re-entry while valid.

9

Lake Minnewanka and Mount Inglismaldie, rising to 2,964 metres on the lake's southern shoreline.

11

Lake Minnewanka is the only lake in Banff National Park on which privately owned power boats are permitted.

WHAT TO DO IN BANFF AND JASPER NATIONAL PARKS

A free interpretive program of conducted walks, evening talks, evening fireside gatherings, slide shows and other events, including special winter activities, helps visitors to learn more about the parks' natural and historical features. Self-guiding nature trails, wayside signs and informative publications are also provided. The natural history museum in the Banff townsite, the interpretive display at Saskatchewan Crossing, exhibits in the Jasper townsite and interpretive displays at the Columbia Icefield are other attractions that visitors can enjoy.
Both parks offer sports activities the year round: swimming, golfing, tennis, horseback riding, raft tours, downhill skiing and cross-country skiing, boat and bus tours, and gondola lifts at Banff and Lake Louise, as well as the Jasper Tramway. There is hot springs bathing in the vicinity of Banff as well as at Miette about 50 km (30 miles) from Jasper.

In Banff and Jasper National Parks, there are a large number of hotels and motels available, as well as youth hostels. Although mainly concentrated in the area of Banff, Lake Louise and Jasper, there are also a few lodges and chalets along the highways through both parks. Since their number is small, early reservations are recommended.

12

Haiduk Lake with the weather-worn slopes and peaks of the Ball Mountain Group, located at the border to British Columbia.

GEOLOGY

During your visit to Banff and Jasper National Parks, you should try to visualize the vast and often violent forces of nature which created the majestic scenes you will see.

A few hundred million years ago much of western North America was an inland sea. For eons, sand, rock and organic sediment built up on the bottom of this sea forming sedimentary rock. Then, beginning about 160 million years ago, the layers of rock on the seabed were pushed up and folded by forces beneath the earth's crust, leaving long, parallel rows of mountains. After the mountains were made, great Ice Age glaciers advanced and retreated, gouging the broad, flat valleys and grinding the peaks to produce their present appearance. Water from melting ice filled the valley lakes. In Jasper National Park, the northward-flowing Athabasca River is the major drainage system through the mountain ranges, while in Banff National Park both the Bow and the North Saskatchewan rivers form the two major drainage systems. The Columbia Icefield, about 125 km (78 miles) north of Lake Louise, may be a remnant of the last great advance.

The Canadian Rockies are just one part of the great mountain system called the Cordillera, which extends along the western edge of both North and South America. In Canada, the Cordillera occupies almost all of British Columbia, southwestern Alberta and the Yukon Territory. In Alberta and southern British Columbia, the Cordillera is made up of two distinct mountain systems: the eastern Cordillera, consisting of Rocky Mountain foothills and the Rocky Mountains, and the western Cordillera, extending out to the Pacific Coast. A wide northwesterly trending valley known as the Rocky Mountain Trench separates these two units; towns such as Invermere, Golden and Radium are found along its length. In the eastern Cordillera, the low rolling foothills extend from the western limit of the prairies near Jumping Pond Creek to the actual mountain front. The Rocky Mountains extend westward to Golden, B. C., in the Rocky Mountain Trench.

The Rockies trend in a southeasterly-northwesterly direction and may be divided into three sub-provinces: the front, the main and the western ranges. The front ranges extend across the eastern part of the two parks, and the main ranges form the peaks of the Continental Divide. The western ranges are all to the west of the parks in British Columbia.

13

Great Gray Owl,
nightwatch of the
Rocky Mountains.

14

Tenting in the wilderness of Banff National Park.

THE SETTLEMENT

Evidence of settlements in areas now inside the parks' boundaries dates back almost 11,000 years. Prehistoric man foraged and hunted for food in the broad valley bottoms and high in the alpine meadows. Remains of Kootenay, Assiniboine and Cree settlements have been found in the parks, and it appears that food was plentiful and the climate favourable for their needs. Life on the land stayed much the same for thousands of years until white men such as David Thompson and Joseph Howse arrived at the beginning of the 19th century, and brought with them the fur trade, and later the Canadian Pacific Railway.

FLORA

The vegetation of Banff and Jasper National Parks can be divided into three major zones: the montane zone, the subalpine zone and the alpine zone. Each of these has characteristic or climax species by which it can be identified.

The montane zone usually occurs at elevations of less than 1,400 metres (4,500 feet), but in Banff National Park, it occurs on warm, dry southwest facing slopes at slightly higher elevations. The soil in these areas is well drained and often has a base of glacial silt. Douglas fir and white spruce are the characteristic trees of this zone.

The subalpine zone with their dense forests occurs from valley bottom to timberline. The typical trees of this zone are Englemann spruce and subalpine fir which grow up to elevations of 2,100 metres (7,000 feet).

The alpine zone, found at elevations above timberline, has a severe climate, with an average yearly temperature of less than –4 °C. The growing season of the plants seldom exceeds 60 days, and there is no predictable frost-free period. Precipitation is high, from 40 to 60

15

Haiduk Valley in the spring with meadows of wild mountain flowers such as Indian Paintbrush.

Cascade Valley in the colours of fall.

inches per year, with most of it occurring as snow.

Alpine plants usually have an abundance of leaves so that they can minimize energy production. Brightly coloured are the alpine flowers. The reds and purples are the most common, which is considered to be beneficial because these colours screen out much of the high ultra-violet radiation in high altitudes.

FAUNA

The wildlife in Banff and Jasper National Parks includes more than 53 species of mammals. They can be separated into three main groups: the small mammals, the hooved animals (or ungulates), and the carnivores (or meat eaters).

SMALL MAMMALS
The small mammals often go by unnoticed, but they can be found almost everywhere. A variety of roots, stems, plants, grasses, berries, herbs and seeds form the mainstay of their diet. The larger of the small mammals add bark and other plant material. They are valuable prey species for the carnivores, as well as for the larger birds. The most common ones are described as follows.

The Chipmunk, whose black stripes on its back extend onto the tip of its nose, is usually found on the ground or in trees.

The Columbian Ground Squirrel, commonly seen in the summer, is rather large with a mottled grey coat and reddish legs. It colonizes grassy areas and its tunnel systems are extensive.

The Golden-Mantled Ground Squirrel is smaller than the Columbian and because of its stripes, is

Park warden on horseback-patrol in the Healy Pass area with British Columbia's Monarch Ramparts.

often mistaken for a large chipmunk, although its stripes do not extend onto its head. It is often located near the edge of rock piles, with its burrows being short and simple.

The Hoary Marmot is a colonial animal inhabiting the alpine area from 1,700 metres (5,500 feet) to 2,400 metres (8,000 feet). Brown in colour with grey hair on its back, it is well known for its high pitched call, and it is often called "whistler." Its den is on hilly ground and usually under a boulder, on which it often can be seen in summer sunning itself.

The Red Squirrels live and nest in coniferous trees. In mid-summer, they cut the tips of cone-bearing branches and store the green cones underground for winter use.

The Porcupine is found in small numbers throughout the subalpine forest. It is nocturnal and spends most of its days sleeping in trees. Like other rodents, porcupines also chew bones and antlers for the minerals contained therein. Contrary to legends, they cannot actually throw their quills, but when cornered, they lash out with their spiny tails.

The Beaver is the largest rodent in the two

parks, and is found in marshy areas at low elevations. Well adapted to aquatic life, the beaver has oily, water-repellent fur, flaps over its eyes and nostrils and a flat rudder-like tail. Beavers build dams to create ponds 1.5 metres to 1.8 metres in depth, in which they build their lodges. They remain active under the ice in winter.

The Muskrat also lives in ponds and marshes and resembles a small beaver except for its long, rat-like tail. It maintains a system of tunnels and canals underneath its lodge-like house along the shoreline.

HOOVED ANIMALS
Hooved animals are large mammals which possess hooves. They are plant-eating, have chambered stomachs and chew their cud. They can be divided into the deer and the sheep and goat families.

The Deer Family
Members of the deer family are distinguished by the fact that the males have antlers made of a bone-like material. The antlers function as symbols of dominance during the mating season and are dropped every year in early spring.

The moose is the largest member of the deer

17

Sunset over Bow Valley
with the towering
silhouette of Castle
Mountain.

Trans-Canada Highway
and Mount Bourgeau
(2,931 m).

family. Distinctive features include long legs, humped shoulders and a flap of skin hanging from the throat called a dewlap. The male carries huge palmed antlers. The moose is a solitary animal which ranges from valley floor to timberline. The preferred habitat in summer is along stream banks and lakeshores where aquatic plants are added to the regular diet of leaves and twigs. Mating season is from mid-September to November, and males are particularly aggressive at this time.

The wapiti (elk) is the second largest member of the deer family. The name wapiti is preferred to avoid confusion with the European moose which is known as "elk." The bulls are characterized by their majestic antlers which may reach from 1.2 to 1.5 metres (4 to 5 feet) in length. Wapiti are gregarious and are primarily grazers who may migrate to higher areas in summer. Grassy areas in the valley bottoms are critical winter habitat.

Mule deer are the characteristic deer of mountains and foothills. Distinctive features are the large ears and blacktipped tail. Mule deer may migrate altitudinally but are commonly found in small groups in drier open areas. The summer diet includes shrubs and broad-leaved plants, and the winter food consists of twigs of evergreens, saplings, and shrubs. Winter range on open slopes and aspen forest is often shared with the wapiti.

Woodland caribou are sighted occasionally in the northern part of Banff National Park, and there is a resident population in Jasper National Park. Caribou are comparable in size to the wapiti, but generally darker in colour. Antlers are often carried by both sexes and are quite variable; however, the presence of a broad brown tine which points downward over the forehead is distinctive. They generally form herds. Lichens are an important food source but grasses, broad-leaved plants and twigs are included in their diet.

The Sheep and Goat Family
Members of the sheep and goat family carry true horns rather than antlers. Horns are carried by both sexes, are permanent, and grow throughout the life of the animal. Horns also serve as symbols of dominance and are sometimes used as weapons.
Bighorn sheep are the second most common ungulate in the parks after the wapiti. They have a sandy coloured coat and a white rump patch. Rams have massive spirally curved horns; the

20

Johnston Canyon's "big" falls; many tourists hike up the Johnston Creek area from the Bow Valley Parkway.

Pharoah Peak (2,723 m), and the sparkling waters of wild Pharoah Creek.

ewe's horns are short and spiky. Bighorns are primarily grazers and migrate seasonally between low grassy slopes and alpine meadows. Escape terrain with rocky ledges is usually nearby. Winter range is very critical and must be on drier slopes where grasses can be pawed through the snow. They are very gregarious and form mixed bands in winter and segregated bands in summer. During mating season, the rams battle for dominance. This is done according to an established ritual of crashing horns together until the weaker animal relinquishes.

Mountain goats are seldom seen because of their preference for steep, rugged habitat, but they are actually quite numerous in the parks; Parks Canada estimates a population of about 1,000 animals. Mountain goats can easily be distinguished from bighorn sheep by their white coats, beards and short black daggerlike horns which are carried by both sexes. If we were to be exact, they are not "goats," but belong to a group of mountain antelopes. Females, or nannies, and their kids often form groups during summer, but males, or billies, are generally solitary. During their rut, fights are rare, but when they do occur, they are vicious. They live on a wide variety of vegetation which allows them to survive year round at elevations above 2,000 metres (6,500 feet).

The wood and plains bison form the final group in the sheep and goat family. Historical accounts indicate that the wood bison once inhabited the mountains, ranging up to timberline. They were similar in appearance and habits to the plains bison, but slightly larger. A captive herd of plains bison was kept in Banff National Park since 1897. They have now been replaced by a small herd of wood bisons.

CARNIVORES
The Carnivores are at the top of the food chain. They are the predators of all the other animals. Well-developed senses, long canine teeth and sharp claws help them to be efficient hunters. Generally, they are meat eaters, but certain groups such as bears have become omnivorous, eating vegetable material as well as meat. Carnivores range in size from the tiny ermine, weighing about 2 ounces, to the grizzly bear reaching a weight of up to 1,000 pounds (450 kilograms).

The Weasel Family
The wolverine is occasionally seen in the subalpine forest and in the alpine tundra and is

River rafting has become a challenging sports activity on Bow River, as well as on Athabasca River in Jasper National Park.

sparsely distributed throughout the parks at all elevations. It is the size of a bear cub and is known as a fighter. The wolverine has a stout muscular body which is dark brown, a short bushy tail and partly retractable claws. Its diet is omnivorous: roots and berries, small mammals, birds and occasionally even sheep. As a scavenger, it cleans up carcasses left by wolves and bears.

The marten is a tree-dweller, has a slender body, large ears and a bushy tail. Colour is usually dark brown. It is a solitary hunter which preys upon moles, mice and especially upon red squirrels. It is not often seen but its tracks can be found on snow. The marten is an abundant species throughout the forested areas of the parks.

The ermine, a ferocious little carnivore, is known for its ability to kill animals larger than itself. It shows a pronounced seasonal variation in colour stimulated by the duration of daylight: in summer, chocolate brown with white under-parts; in winter, completely white except for a black tip on the tail. Its diet includes mice, shrews, birds, squirrels and the occasional porcupine.

The long-tailed weasel is slightly larger than the ermine and has a longer tail. Its habits are similar as is its prey. It is less common than the ermine.

The Dog Family

The coyote is a medium-sized dog with a slender muzzle, large pointed ears, and a bushy tail usually held downwards. The family pack – parents and offspring – is the basic social unit. Coyotes are shy nocturnal scavengers who patrol the highway and railway in search of road kills. They are also active predators of small rodents and birds; deer may be felled by teamwork. They must be on the alert for larger predators such as the wolf, cougar, black and grizzly bears. Their nocturnal serenades are often heard, particularly in late August, when the pups leave the den to join the family pack.

The wolf is similar in appearance to a large German Shepherd but is lankier with longer legs and larger feet. Its muzzle is larger and less pointed than that of a coyote. Colour varies from beige to brown, grey to black. The dark wolves are predominant in the mountains of Alberta and British Columbia. Their long quivering howl is distinctive. The family pack consists of parents, offspring and close relatives. There is a definite social hierarchy within the

23

Larch Valley, golden in the fall, is the first mountain valley through which an exciting trail leads from Moraine Lake via Sentinel Pass into Paradise Valley, and further on to Lake Louise.

24

Cougars, or mountain lions, the largest Canadian cats, can still be found in the remote backcountry of the Rockies.

pack and only the dominant male and female mate. They are primarily hunters of big game. Wapiti (elk), moose, deer and bighorn sheep appear to be the important prey. The wolf has no natural predators.

The fox has a slim body and a very bushy tail. Its thick fur is brown, or red-brown, and its social unit is the family pack. Its mating season is the winter time. It preys on small mammals such as chipmunks and squirrels. The red fox is the most common species in this area, but there are several other kinds living in the northern parts of the continent.

The Cat Family
The mountain lion or cougar is the largest Canadian cat. Its body is long and lithe, its head small and its tail about 76 cm (30 inches) long. The adult colour is predominantly light brown, with a white throat and chest. The cougar is solitary, nocturnal and rarely seen. Its lair is usually in a rocky crevice or in the shelter of a windfall. The cougar hunts by stalking and pouncing much like a domestic cat. Members of the deer family are their favourite food, but sheep, goats and small mammals are also hunted.

The lynx is a medium-sized cat with a short body, stubby tail and large feet which facilitate travel on snow. The fur is long, thick and mainly grey in colour. A prominent ruff surrounds the face. The lynx preys upon small animals such as rodents, hare and birds. They can rarely be seen in the parks.

The Bear Family
Two types of bears inhabit the parks: the black bear and the grizzly bear. Both are omnivorous in diet, plants forming the mainstay of their food, supplemented by carrion and whatever small animals they manage to kill. Winter estivation is characteristic for the bear family, and they live off fat layers built up during the summer months. Mating occurs in summer, but the embryo does not begin development until late fall and only if the sow is fat and in good condition, ensuring strong offspring. Bears suckle their tiny cubs throughout the winter months. They have poor eyesight but their hearing and their sense of smell are acute. They are not naturally aggressive, but their behaviour is highly unpredictable. All bears are potentially dangerous to man. Those animals which forage on human food or garbage become habituated to man and, as a result, less fearful; thus they are even more dangerous to visitors.

25

Scenic Moraine Lake in the Valley of The Ten Peaks.

Avalanche off Victoria Glacier above the frozen Lake Louise.

Deepsnow downhill skiing on the slopes of Mount Whitehorn in the Lake Louise area.

The black bear is commonly seen in forested areas, along roadsides and in campgrounds. It is smaller than the grizzly, lacks a hump on its shoulders and has a straight facial profile. Colour varies from black to cinnamon. White patches on the chest are not uncommon. They have short curved claws and are agile tree climbers. Black bears have few enemies but will vacate any area frequented by grizzlies. Summer migrations are minimal, and the black bears usually stay below timberline.

The grizzly bear is unmistakable because of the large muscular hump on its shoulders. Its fur is long and thick. Colour varies but is usually light brown with some blond or white hairs giving a grizzled or silver-tip effect. Claws are long and slender (about six inches), and are used for digging (thereby dulling), preventing an adult grizzly from climbing trees. They show pronounced migration, spending summer in the alpine areas and descending to the valleys in spring and fall when food is scarce. As a supplement to their plant diet, hibernating marmots and ground squirrels are often excavated in the fall; big game such as wapiti (elk) and their young are occasionally felled. Winter dens are located at about 2,100 metres (7,000 feet) on the northeastward slopes. In

these areas, deep-snow accumulation provides an ideal insulation. Grizzly sows are extremely protective of their young, which are born during the winter months, and may attack if threatened or fearful. As with black bears, the cubs stay with their mother for just over a year.

Hints for Hiking in Bear Country
When hiking in areas frequented by bears, the best strategy is to warn the animals of your presence by carrying "bear bells" or making loud noises such as clapping or shouting. Since bears are shy by nature, they will·usually vacate the area immediately. Avoid travelling in an upwind direction or in areas of poor visibility.
If you do sight a bear, the best reaction is to slowly walk away rather than running which may provoke a charge. In the case of sighting a grizzly bear, you could also climb up a large tree, since the adults cannot climb after you. However, be sure it is a grizzly and not a black bear, since the black bear is a fast and able climber. In a rare case where all these precautions fail and a sudden attack occurs, your best chance is to lie on the ground and "play dead."

Lake Louise, gem of the Canadian Rocky Mountains, attracts millions of visitors from all over the world.

BIRDS

There are many resident birds in the parks; four of the most commonly seen ones are members of the crow family: the Gray Jay, Clark's Nutcracker, Black-billed Magpie, and the raven. Others include the osprey; the fish hawk with its grey colour above and its white below; and the bald eagle, which when mature has a wingspan of up to 2.3 metres (7.5 feet) and may be distinguished from golden eagles by their white heads and tails. While bald eagles nest near water in large trees, the golden eagle is often seen soaring at high elevations and nests on inaccessible cliffs in the backcountry areas of the parks.

FISH

The lakes and rivers of Banff and Jasper National Parks also support fair-sized fish populations. Here you will find the Rocky Mountain whitefish and several species of trout as well as other kinds.

BANFF NATIONAL PARK

The early beginnings of Banff stretch far back into the pages of time, most of it shrouded in Indian lore and legend. Only the footsteps of the white man have been traced with some degree of accuracy.

David Thompson, one of Canada's earliest explorers of the Rocky Mountains, arrived in 1880 at the Gap about 31 km (19 miles) east of today's townsite of Banff. Thompson belonged to the corps of map makers and fur traders of the North West Company, those legendary daring men who in the decades before and after 1800 explored the entire Canadian west as far north as the Arctic and as far south as the American West. (The North West Company was absorbed by the Hudson's Bay Company, the older fur-trading company, in 1821.)

In 1807, David Thompson returned to the Rockies by canoe on the North Saskatchewan River and crossed the mountains on horseback at the Howse Pass, with only 1,500 metres (4,900 feet), the lowest point in the ridge of the Continental Divide within the central Rocky Mountains. Following the path of two North West Company's voyageurs named LeBlanc and LaGassi, he travelled on and built Kootenay House, the first fur-trading post on the Columbia

Crowfoot Glacier, sitting high in the mountains over the southern part of Bow Lake, feeding the lake with blue-green glacial waters.

River.

August of 1841 saw the arrival of Banff's first tourist: Sir George Simpson, governor of the fur empire of the Hudson's Bay Company, accompanied by the Stoney Indian guide Peechee. His route, part of a round-the-world-trip, led him through Devil's Gap, along Lake Minnewanka to the Bow Valley. He crossed over the pass named after him and over the Sinclair as well.

Then followed James Sinclair, Father Pierre de Smet – a Jesuit missionary, who came north from the Oregon territory via Whiteman Pass to preach to the Blackfoot Indians – and a Wesleyan missionary named Robert T. Rundle, who journeyed to the foot of Cascade Mountain and held services for the Stoney Indians on the shore of Lake Minnewanka.

In 1858, Dr. James Hector, surgeon and geologist, staff of the Palliser Expedition, explored the Bow Valley and much of the surrounding area. Hector was the first white man known to cross Vermilion and Kicking Horse Passes.

Then came the Canadian Pacific Railway. In 1881 Major A. B. Rogers, an American surveyor hired by the CPR, located the Rogers Pass over the Selkirk Mountains and continued preliminary survey work through the Kicking Horse Pass and in the Bow Valley. Rogers was assisted by Tom Wilson, the famous packer and outfitter supplying the survey crews, who discovered Lake Louise in 1882. While the railway had pushed its way through the Bow Valley past Siding 29 (Banff) and to Laggan Station (Lake Louise) in 1883 – today remembered as the birthdate of Banff – two other railway workers, Frank McCabe and William McCardell, discovered the Cave and Basin Hot Springs in the same year. The commercial value of the springs was recognized and rough bath houses were soon erected. As the two men had not made a formal claim, an ownership dispute arose when several other men laid claim to the spring. The legal battle that followed brought the hot springs to the attention of the CPR and the federal government. In 1885, an order-in-council established a 26-square-km (ten-square-mile) national area as the Banff Hot Springs Reserve for the "sanitary advantage of the public," thereby being the predecessor of what later became Banff National Park.

In 1985 the park will celebrate its 100 years of heritage conservation. The "official" date of birth of Canada's first national park was only two years later when the survey report of the Hot Springs Reserve, compiled by George A. Stewart,

Grizzly bears can often be seen during the summer in the alpine areas of the Rockies.

described much of the surrounding country as very scenic and suitable for a protected area. The final survey encompassed an area of 673 square km (260 square miles), extending from Sulphur Mountain to the end of Lake Minnewanka, and the federal government's legislation established Rocky Mountains Park for which Stewart was appointed the first park superintendent.

The legislation of this park was modelled very closely after that of Yellowstone National Park in the United States, which had been created 15 years earlier. Similar to today's policy, the Rocky Mountains Park was to be "a public park and pleasure ground for the advantage, benefit, and enjoyment of the people of Canada," and that no leases, licenses or permits would be issued that could "impair the usefulness of the park for purposes of public enjoyment and recreation." Later on the park area was enlarged, decreased and again enlarged. Now Banff National Park encompasses an area of 6,641 square km (2,564 square miles).

Banff National Park offers more than 1,300 km (810 miles) of trails for hiking and cross-country skiing. The trails wind through the mountainous backcountry, being by far the best, and the healthiest, way to enjoy the park. Printed guides are available at the information centres at no cost.

The highest peak in Banff Park is Mount Forbes at 3,628 metres (11,902 feet). Named after Dr. James D. Forbes, a Scottish scientist, the mountain is located in the northwest portion of the park, southwest of Glacier Lake. It is followed by a large number of other mountains, especially those along the Continental Divide, which count not much less in altitude.

The administrative and cultural centre of the park is the town of Banff, located 16 km (10 miles) inside the east gate. It is nestled at the junction of the valleys of the Bow and Spray rivers at an altitude of 1,383 metres (4,538 feet). The town of 4,000 inhabitants is surrounded by such distinctive landmarks as Cascade Mountain, at 2,998 metres (9,836 feet), the second highest mountain around the town, known by the Indians as "Stoney Chief." It is surely the most frequently photographed mountain, its panorama visible the length of Banff Avenue.

White Spruce

Englemann Spruce

Black Spruce

Lodgepole Pine

Limber Pine

Whitebark Pine

Douglas Fir

Subalpine Fir

Alpine Larch

Trembling Aspen

Balsam Poplar

Black Cottonwood

Trees in Banff
and Jasper
National Parks

The Waterfowl Lakes alongside of the Icefields Parkway with towering Mount Chephren (3,266 m), named after the Egyptian Pharaoh of the fourth dynasty.

Moose can often be seen in this area, such as this bull moose walking through the waters of Mistaya Lake, with Mount Murchison (3,333 m) to the north.

Beautiful turquoise-coloured Peyto Lake, surrounded by the dense and healthy forests of the valley floor along the Icefields Parkway.

Mount Rundle, the highest peak, stands dramatically on guard over Rundle Gap above Bow Falls, and clouds spill off its razor-sharp ridge at 2,999 metres (9,838 feet). Sulphur Mountain's heavily wooded slopes rise to 2,450 metres (8,040 feet). At its top a visitor can enjoy a magnificent panoramic view from the new restaurant with its full 360° observation terrace, after riding in an eight-minute lift aboard the gondola. It takes only seven minutes by gondola lift to the "Cliffhouse" on the side of Mount Norquay to catch a view of the snow-covered peaks of the Fairholme Range in the distance with its Mount Girouard of 2,995 m (9,825 feet) and its Mount Inglismaldie with a slightly lower altitude. Mount Norquay with its peak rising to 2,522 m (8,275 feet) is at the same time home of Banff's famous ski slopes. Some years ago, another downhill skiing area was developed, the Sunshine Village ski area, located outside Banff to the west and southwest. It can be reached from the parking lot by the gondola, sloping down from Goat's Eye Mountain and Lookout Mountain.

Banff has a multitude of hotel and motel accommodation, although in the peak travel season in July and August many of them are full. The "Queen" of all is Banff Springs Hotel, the oldest in the Rocky Mountains of Canada. Close by the hot springs, the CPR built this huge and luxurious hotel. William Van Horne, first construction manager and later president of the CPR, was one of the first to realize the potential of this area for tourists from all over the world. Begun in 1886, the hotel complex was completed in 1888. Due to the rising number of summer and winter tourists, the hotel had to be expanded between 1900 and 1910. Later, in 1926, it was struck by fire, and the new hotel, as it exists now, was completed in 1928.

Banff is also the home of the Banff School of Fine Arts, established in 1933, and now known as the Banff Centre.

There are numerous excellent walks, short hikes and drives in the vicinity of Banff. Some examples include the Fenland Self-Guiding Trail, the Hoodos Nature Trail, the Sundance Canyon Trail, the Spray River Trail, the Rundle Mountain Trail, the Cascade Amphitheatre Trail, the Elk Lake Trail, the Edith Pass Trail, the Stony Squaw Trail, the Upper Bankhead Trail, the Lake Minnewanka Trail, the Johnson Lake Trail and a number of others. Literature pertaining to these trails is available at the information centres.

One of the longest trails is the Lake Minnewanka Trail with an average hiking time of seven to ten hours, starting out at the western end of the lake. It follows the north shore of the lake

Columbia Icefield's Saskatchewan Glacier, flowing down through the long narrow valley between Mount Saskatchewan (3,342 m) and Mount Athabasca (3,491 m), is the main source of the North Saskatchewan River.

underneath the mighty Mount Aylmer of an altitude of 3,162 metres (10,375 feet). Lake Minnewanka is the largest in Banff National Park, and it, having been named by Indians in 1888, means "Lake of the Water Spirit." It had also carried the name Devil's or Devil's Head Lake and, even before that, it was named Peechee Lake by George Simpson in 1841. At the turn of the century Lake Minnewanka was much smaller than it is today. The old resort town of Minnewanka Landing had to be given up when Banff needed more electricity, since the powerhouse at Bankhead, one of the oldest coal mining operations in the west, did not produce enough. In 1912, a small dam was constructed at the outlet of Lake Minnewanka. In 1924, when the Bankhead operation was finally closed, the government authorized construction of a new powerhouse at the site of the original Lake Minnewanka dam to meet the increasing demand in the Banff area. In 1941 the hydroelectric facilities were greatly expanded, and a new much larger dam was constructed, raising the water level of the lake by another 18 metres (60 feet) so that presently the lake's water level is about 27 metres (90 feet) above its original waterline, and its size has been enlarged thereby to about 19 km (12 miles) by 1.5 to 3 km (1 to 2 miles).

When you drive west, it is recommendable to use Highway 1A, also known as the Bow Valley Parkway, a scenic alternative to the busy Trans-Canada Highway.

After about 16 km (10 miles) you will reach Johnston Canyon; a short hike from the parking area takes you to the Lower Falls. Sturdy walkways to the Upper Falls carry you over a rushing torrent that flows between the walls of the deep canyon. A most peculiar bird lives here. It is called the water Ouzel, or the "dipper," after its habit of swimming, diving, and even walking on the bottom of the stream to feed. Beyond the canyon are the Ink Pots, seven cold-water springs, two of which are of blue-green colour caused by the spring action of the water up through the silt and quicksand.

A short distance from the Johnston Canyon comes Castle Mountain, formerly called Mount Eisenhower after Dwight D. Eisenhower, the American general and president. Before the end of World War II it carried the same name as today because the mountain was actually a short mountain range, resembling the shape of a mighty castle, rising up to an altitude of 2,862 metres (9,390 feet). Looking southwest from Castle-Junction above the Bow River and the dense valley forests, the Banff Windermere Highway branches off the Trans-Canada

Athabasca Glacier, flowing down from Columbia Icefield, is the first attraction for visitors entering Jasper National Park from the south, and it is the feeding glacier for the Sunwapta River.

Bighorn sheep can frequently be watched right on or beside the Icefields Parkway.

Mountain goats can often be seen in the higher slopes of the mountains in this area.

Highway and, following the valleys of the Vermilion and Kootenay rivers, reaches another famous Hot Springs Resort, Radium Hot Springs, B. C., at the southern end of Kootenay National Park.

Discovered by Tom Wilson, Lake Louise, gem of the Rocky Mountain lakes is at an altitude of 1,725 metres (5,660 feet).
One night, when Wilson was camped with a packtrain at Laggan Station, he heard the thunderous crashes of avalanches from above, and asking one of the Stoney Indians nearby about the noise, he was told that it came from "the lake of little fishes." Led by the Stoney, Wilson was the first white man to sit on the shores of Lake Louise in 1882. "For some time we sat and smoked and gazed at the gem of beauty beneath the glacier," Wilson remembered. The colour of the water inspired him to name it Emerald Lake, although the name was later changed to Louise by the Geographic Board in honour of Princess Louise Caroline Alberta, daughter of England's Queen Victoria, and wife of the Marquis of Lorne, then the governor general of Canada.
In 1890 the original Chateau (Chalet) was built at Lake Louise by the CPR. It was the second Canadian Pacific Railway hotel in the Rocky

Mountains. Also destroyed by fire in 1924, its reconstruction resulted in the Chateau Lake Louise as it stands today. Being similarly luxurious as the Banff Springs Hotel and located right at the shores of Lake Louise, it has become a favourite temporary homestead for the wealthier tourists. In 1892, a 132-square-km (a 51-square-mile) reserve was set aside by the federal government. The Lake Louise Reservation was incorporated into Rocky Mountain Park in 1902.
The village of Lake Louise has basically remained as it was; a railway station in the Bow Valley, surrounded by a few service facilities such as a post office, a few gas stations, one or two grocery stores and not much more. But the millions of visitors passing through on the Trans-Canada Highway, and those who stay for a while, will find, in addition to the Chateau, a number of other hotel and motel accommodations located as close as possible to the lake itself.
When you board Mount Whitehorn's gondola which, as one of Canada's longest, brings you up to an elevation of over 2,000 metres (6,680 feet), you have a spectacular view over the whole Lake Louise panorama. You will see the lake itself with Mount Victoria whose peak rises up to 3,464 metres (11,365 feet) and on the left

This region in the Sunwapta Valley with the river still young is often referred to as "The Beauty Spot;" perhaps because it is indeed very scenic or since it is at this point where the Beauty Creek flows into the Sunwapta.

Mount Fairview as well as mighty Mount Temple with an altitude of 3,547 metres (11,636 feet), the highest mountain in the Bow Range.

The trails beginning at Lake Louise are manifold. Hiking trails up to Lakes Mirror and Agnes bring you to an elevation of 2,125 metres (6,972 feet) from where you can trail on to the Plain of Six Glaciers, an unforgettable scenery of blue ice, crawling down the mountain surfaces.

Moraine Lake at an altitude of about 1,900 metres (6,230 feet) can also be reached on a hike of more than 15 km (9.5 miles) through the Paradise Valley, then via the Sentinel Pass and through Larch Valley, or via the Moraine Valley on a more direct route. The trail via the Saddle Pass and Paradise Valley is one of the most spectacular ones in the entire Rocky Mountains of Canada, but it is only good for the younger, and the healthier, hikers. Moraine Lake can also be reached comfortably by automobile on the Moraine Lake Road.

Moraine Lake with its azure-blue water, still frozen in June, is located in the Valley of the Ten Peaks, and is set before a backdrop of sharp, glaciated summits called the Wenkchemna Peaks – the Stoney Indian word for ten – hence the Valley of the Ten Peaks, all of which are above the 3,000-metre (10,000-feet) level. As author Brian Patton described the lake: "Moraine Lake

would appear to be the creation of a rockslide from the Tower of Babel, rising immediately above the northeast end of the lake. The lake received its name from its first visitor, who mistakenly thought the large pile of boulders near the outlet to be a terminal moraine." The azure blue of Moraine Lake is a result of melting glaciers, and the area surrounding the lake offers another two spectacular hikes; one to the lower Consolation Lake, and the other to Eiffel Lake. To accommodate the tired or hungry traveller the Moraine Lake Lodge alongside of Moraine Lake has recently been built. The whole Moraine Lake area is, depending on the snow conditions, open to the public between early June and mid-October.

In winter one of the major attractions of Lake Louise is skiing, which began to evolve here over 50 years ago. Back in the 1930s, a small ski chalet was built 19 km (12 miles) north of Lake Louise at an altitude of 2,100 metres (7,000 feet). Situated on the banks of Little Pipestone Creek, it is located in the centre of magnificent ski touring country. Skoki Ski Lodge was the first of its kind in the Canadian Rockies, and it is still there today.

A second winter sports accommodation was erected in 1937: the two-storey Mount Temple Chalet at the entrance to the Ptarmigan Valley

Tangle Creek bumps over rocky ledges right down to the Icefields Parkway and joins the Sunwapta River on its way north to the Athabasca River.

Scenic Astoria Valley leads from the Athabasca Valley in a westerly direction to the Amethyst Lakes and Tonquin Valley on the western boundary of Jasper National Park.

and only five miles from Lake Louise station, which as well is a popular lodge for skiers. As the skiing area around Lake Louise became more popular, and the demand for downhill skiing increased, a gondola was constructed on Mount Whitehorn in 1958, opening an area of great slopes. In the 1960s, an additional chairlift was added and two famous runs, the "Olympic Men's Downhill" and the "Olympic Ladies' Downhill." These runs, cut into Mount Whitehorn's snow-covered slopes, are famous the world over.

A short distance west of Lake Louise, where the Trans-Canada Highway proceeds on via the Kicking Horse Pass into British Columbia's Yoho National Park, you are entering Highway No. 93. It is the famed Icefields Parkway, whose 230 km (143 miles) to Jasper run in a northwesterly direction through the wide valleys of the Bow, the North Saskatchewan, the Sunwapta and Athabasca rivers. Alongside of the chain of tall peaks of the Rocky Mountain's main ranges and its huge icefields and glaciers to the left is certainly the most spectacular stretch of highway in Canada's west.

The Wapta, the Columbia, the Chaba, the Clemenceau and the Hooker Icefields, spread over the wide shoulders of mountain ranges along the Continental Divide and all at altitudes of over 3,000 metres (10,000 feet), which spill out hundreds of mighty glaciers to the east, north, and west of the Great Divide. The Columbia Icefield, at an area of 325 square km (125 square miles), the largest in the Rocky Mountains, feeds eight large glaciers, three of which – the Athabasca, the Dome, and the Stutfield – can be seen from the parkway. It is also the Columbia Icefield, which reaches a depth of 600 to 900 metres (2,000 to 3,000 feet), whose glacial outlets feed river-systems reaching three different oceans, the Nelson and North Saskatchewan to the Atlantic via Hudson's Bay, the Sunwapta and Athabasca via the Mackenzie to the Arctic Ocean, and the Bush and Columbia to the Pacific. For the last 150 to 200 years all of the glacier-toes in the Rocky Mountains have been retreating, since under the current climatic conditions the supply of ice does not equal the summer melt. The Athabasca Glacier, for instance, is receding about 14 metres (46 feet) each year in present times.

Gas, accommodation and other services are available in only a few places along the Icefields Parkway. Travellers should check the map and plan the trip accordingly. There are, however, many campgrounds and picnic areas along the way.

Black bears are agile climbers.

Mighty Athabasca Falls, where a rainbow shines over the clear, sparkling waters that thunder down into a steep-walled canyon.

42

Flock of Canada geese migrating to southern quarters in winter.

While cruising northwest on the parkway, you will see on your left the peaks of the Waputik Range with an altitude of around 2,700 metres (9,000 feet), bordered on its northern end by Hector Lake, named after James Hector of the Palliser Expedition, and opposite it to the east Mt. Hector, whose peak reaches 3,394 metres (11,135 feet). Then, again on the left is scenic Bow Lake, its western shoreline caged in by the steep walls of the Crowfoot Mountain. Towards Bow Lake's southern end the Crowfoot Glacier is visible, and on its northwestern side the visitors get a glance of Bow Glacier, whose falls can be reached on a comfortable trail. The Num-Ti-Jah Lodge invites the traveller for a rest.

The Bow River follows the parkway uphill for another few miles almost to the Bow Pass of 2,070 metres (6,800 feet). As the road declines again, you will soon see another picturesque mountain lake, Peyto Lake, opening up a magnificent view into the wide valley of the Mistaya River to the north. It is recommended to stop here for a while and walk the trail which leads to a viewpoint above the lake, offering a wonderful Rocky Mountain panorama, unsurpassed by many others.

The lake received its unusual name after Bill Peyto, who at the turn of the century had explored this area and was later appointed to become one of the early park wardens of Banff National Park.

Being fed by Peyto Glacier of the Wapta Icefield, its northernmost end narrows into the Mistaya River, whose Indian name means "great or grizzly bear." It accompanies the parkway around Mount Patterson at an altitude of 3,197 metres (10,490 feet) to Mistaya Lake. The lake is hardly visible from the road. It waters into Waterfowl Lakes, where you can admire the towering peaks of Mount Chephren, 3,266 metres (10,715 feet), and Mount Howse, 3,292 metres (10,800 feet). Mount Chephren was named after an Egyptian Pharaoh from the fourth dynasty around the year 2700 B.C., and does indeed resemble the shape of a pyramid.

A few miles further you will see a sign advising you that from here a trail is leading to the Mistaya Canyon, where between steep crude walls the river plunges down deep into sparkling blue colour. A small bridge is crossing the canyon at its end, leading to another trail to the Sarbach Lookout Point on Mount Sarbach's northern slopes. There is a further trail nearby, which guides the hiker on to historical grounds, to the Howse River which, like the Mistaya River, reaches the North Saskatchewan River a few miles downstream. This was the route that David Thompson took in 1807. He arrived from

43

Packtrain, returning from a camp in Tonquin Valley.

the east by canoe on the North Saskatchewan and continued on by canoe and horse up the river valley of the Howse until he crossed the Continental Divide at a pass route, which later was named Howse Pass. Both river and pass received their names after Joseph Howse, another agent of the North West Company, who followed David Thomson's route only three years later.

To follow Thompson's first trading route through the Rocky Mountains is certainly worthwhile. From the Mistaya River to Howse Pass at the B. C. border, where the legendary Blaeberry River has its origin, is a hiking distance of about 30 km (19 miles) along the valley of the Howse River, which means a two-day trip. Hikers need to carry with them suitable overnight equipment. But it certainly is one of the most exciting alpine hikes, between the mighty mountain massives of Mounts Sarbach, Chephren and Howse to the east and those of Mounts Outram, David and Strahan and Convey on the western side of the trail, all peaks towering over 3,000 metres (10,000 feet). Close by is Mount Forbes, which is hidden behind the previously mentioned mountains to the west. After passing the Saskatchewan Crossing where Highway 11 – the David Thompson Highway – branches off to the east through the lovely

Rocky Mountain Forest Reserve to Red Deer, the Icefields Parkway follows the North Saskatchewan River upstream between the towering peaks of Mounts Wilson, Amery, Coleman and Saskatchewan. North of these the Columbia Icefield's Saskatchewan Glacier gives life to the river of the same name in a long, stretched valley. It can be hiked into comfortably from the 250° curve of the parkway, as it climbs up steeply towards Sunwapta Pass, whose summit, at an altitude of 2,035 metres (6,680 feet), is the borderline to Jasper National Park.

Maligne Canyon, where
the Maligne River
surges 50 metres down
between narrow
limestone walls.

Athabasca Valley in the
fall colours of
trembling aspens,
looking south.

Park warden's
Avalanche Gun Tower,
watching and
protecting the Marmot
Basin ski area in the
vicinity of Jasper.

Lone skier in the serenity of the early morning sun at Eight Pass.

JASPER NATIONAL PARK

Surprisingly, Alberta's north was commercially developed ahead of the south, with Fort Edmonton already established as a fur-trading post in 1795. Missionaries rather than fur traders and map makers led the way into the south, establishing schools and churches, and good relations with the Indians. In fact, Father Albert Lacombe helped negotiate the agreement with the Blackfoot Nation in 1880 making it possible to build Canada's first transcontinental railway through the mountains via Banff and Lake Louise.

The voyageurs and explorers of the Hudson's Bay and North West Company, such as Alexander Mackenzie and David Thompson, first searched for a gateway to the west through the Rocky Mountains. Besides these well-known names, the French-Canadian voyageurs, tough and wilderness-proven, were carrying the main load of the two companies' explorations in the west. Hence there appear many French names in northern Alberta as well as in the Jasper area; names such as Miette, Barbette, Maligne, Brulé, Brazeau and Tête Jaune, the original name of the pass leading to British Columbia which was later renamed the Yellowhead Pass.

David Thompson, exploring and mapping the west since 1789, had found the more southern route up the North Saskatchewan and Howse rivers in 1807, but he and his men had encountered trouble from Indian tribes in British Columbia. He attempted then to find another path through the Rocky Mountains. Travelling from Fort Edmonton and up the Athabasca River into the mountains, they rested in the large valley where the Miette River flows into the Athabasca. Here was built the first permanent habitation in 1811. One of Thompson's men, William Henry, was left behind at Old Fort Point while Thompson and the others pushed on up the Athabasca, branched off into the Whirlpool River to the west, bringing them due north of the Hooker Icefield to another low elevation point of the Continental Divide and beyond that into British Columbia. This route became famous as the route of the North West and Hudson's Bay Company fur brigades; the Athabasca Pass being used for 50 years as the main path through the mountains.

The tired voyageurs carrying their loads of fur would stop overnight at Old Fort Point's Henry House, the post built by William Henry as he awaited Thompson's return. This was the root of the settlement, known today as Jasper. Its name was derived from Jasper Hawes, a long-time clerk at another fur brigade way-station

49

Athabasca River spring
break-up.

A new winter fun in
the Jasper area is dog
sled travelling.

51

Red Fox, predator of small mammals such as ground squirrels.

located 32 km (20 miles) downstream from Jasper at the Athabasca, which was built in 1813. Fur trading declined after 1850, and there were few travellers in the area until the Grand Trunk Pacific Railway arrived 60 years later. But adventurers and mountaineers trickled through; people such as Paul Kane, the artist, and the Overlanders, a group of 250 men, women and children, had come from the east on a most strenuous journey to Jasper in 1862 in order to rest and prepare themselves for the continuation of their trip to the gold fields of the "Wild Caribou" in British Columbia. Their journey by foot up the Miette River Valley and via the Yellowhead Pass into British Columbia, where one group of them built log rafts to travel the Fraser River and another, a smaller group, searched for the North Thompson River, is well known in Canada's western history. Other travellers passing through Jasper included Mary Schäffer, the woman who followed old Indian trails to hitherto-unknown Maligne Lake. Jasper National Park was founded in 1907, a great block of widely unexplored wilderness.

The park encompasses an area of 10,878 square km (4,200 square miles) and offers more than 1,000 km (620 miles) of trails for hiking and cross-country skiing. Today, in spite of its two highways and its railroad, which has long been overtaken by the Canadian National Railways, the park looks very much like it did when David Thompson first saw it.

Approaching on the Icefields Parkway from the south, the first stop, just a few miles beyond Sunwapta Pass, is the Icefield Centre with the comfortable Columbia Icefield Chalet. As the Athabasca Glacier stretches its toe closely towards the parkway, it is only a ten-minute walk, however chilly, to reach Sunwapta Lake and the glacier itself. In addition to this, you can drive, hike or take a tour bus uphill a small winding road beside the southern edge of Athabasca Glacier to a terminal, and there get a 45-minute tour aboard one of the several huge "snowmobiles." They travel five miles across this "ancient river of ice" and the driver-guides are usually quite knowledgeable, explaining to their passengers about icefields, glaciers and their particulars. The snowmobile terminal is nestled against the northern side of Mount Athabasca, whose peak reaches an altitude of 3,491 metres (11,452 feet). Topping that is Alberta's highest

Medicine Lake, a unique geological phenomenon, is filled with the waters of Maligne River in summer; in fall and winter the lake disappears, as the waters of the "sinking river" vanish into the lake bottom.

point of elevation, Mount Columbia at 3,747 metres (12,294 feet). Many exciting hiking trails, such as those to Wilcox Pass, to Parker Ridge, to Nigel Pass and to other destinations, are available, but the visitor should be aware of the chilly winds that blow down from the many glaciers of the Columbia Icefield in the west, even in summer.

A few miles north on the parkway, you are bound to see bighorn sheep close by or on the highway. They are used to people, but you should always remember that they are also wild animals. It is likely that, a short distance further, mountain goats are climbing and grazing on the lower slopes of Wilcox Peak. And shortly thereafter you will notice the lovely Tangle Falls right at the parkway, its waters rushing underneath the road towards Sunwapta River, which has accompanied the travellers since the Icefield Centre.

Following the Sunwapta to the north, the parkway is accompanied in the west by towering peaks and glacial areas of the Winston Churchill Range. At the northern end of the Range visitors can make a left turn to reach the Sunwapta Falls on a short access road. A footbridge affords thrilling views into a deep right-angled canyon where the Sunwapta River turns a corner to plunge towards the Athabasca River. From here on, the Athabasca Valley widens pleasantly.

When a lake with the romantic name of Honeymoon Lake is passed, Mount Christie appears over the western shores of Athabasca River, followed by Mount Fryatt, at 3,361 metres (11,026 feet) the tallest in this part of Jasper Park. A short distance thereafter, Highway 93A branches off from the Icefields Parkway, leading a few hundred yards to the magnificent Athabasca Falls, where the river thunders down into a steep-walled canyon. Highway 93A, a section of the first Banff-Jasper road, was opened to automobile traffic in 1940. It follows the river, parallelling the Icefield Parkway on the river's western side. When the road gets hilly again, you are approaching Astoria Valley, where a narrow and winding road guides you uphill towards famous Mount Edith Cavell with its dramatically and powerfully steep northeastern slope, rising to its top at 3,363 metres (11,032 feet). From the parking lot, there are trails passing through portions of the upper valley of Cavell Creek, which was covered with glacial ice as recently as the turn of the century. Time and energy allowing, it is worth your while to proceed on the trail to the Cavell

Canoeing on beautiful Maligne Lake, the largest glacier-fed lake in the Canadian Rockies, with Llysfran Peak (3,141 m) and Mount Mary Vaux (3,201 m) on its western shores.

Maligne Lake Road
with the first October
snow, accompanied by
long ridges of the
Queen Elizabeth
Ranges.

Bull moose can be frequently seen on the meadows of Maligne River valley.

meadows at treeline and the alpine region beyond. Along the path, there are spectacular views of Angel Glacier, sitting high on the side of Mount Edith Cavell. The upper section of the trail may still be under snow in early summer, but by mid-July a beautiful display of mountain wild flowers can be seen here, as well as hoary marmots, pika and ptarmigan. At a viewpoint across the valley from Angel Glacier, you should stop to catch your breath while listening and watching for avalanches on Mount Edith Cavell. The mountain with its steep walls is a challenge for mountain climbers from all over, offering the triumph of the most thrilling panoramic views from the top.

You are approaching the town of Jasper soon after you have reached Highway 93 A again, which meets Highway 93, the Icefields Parkway, not long thereafter. A few miles later, the parkway, ends at the intersection with Highway 16, the Yellowhead Highway, which, to the west, connects with Prince George and Prince Rupert. Via Highway 5 you can reach the Trans-Canada Highway again at Kamloops, proceeding to Vancouver and Victoria; to the east, Highway 16 connects with Edmonton, Saskatoon, Yorkton and Portage la Prairie, located just west of Winnipeg.

Jasper with a population of close to 4,000, located in a wide valley where the Miette and Maligne rivers flow into the Athabasca River and surrounded by lakes and forests, is the centre of Jasper National Park, whose boundary to the north or northwest is yet another almost 115 km (70 miles) away. However, it can be reached only by hiking and is left to the young and healthy, and to the park wardens.

Jasper offers the summer and winter tourist just about any attraction and entertainment one can think of. Besides a good assortment of hotels and motels, there is the beautifully located Jasper Park Lodge, a CN hotel complex. Jasper has its "Tramway" up to the high slopes of The Whistlers, overlooking the whole valley and surrounding mountain chains and ranges. It offers to the winter visitor the Marmot Basin ski area with five chairlifts and T-Bars from December to April. Parks Canada has built numerous magnificent walking and hiking trails near the town, such as those to Lakes Patricia and Pyramid, the Saturday Night Lake Circle, the trail to the Valley of Five Lakes and the one to Maligne Canyon.

From Jasper, there are four excursions that are a "must." One excursion leads you towards the eastern gate of the park up to Pocahontas on

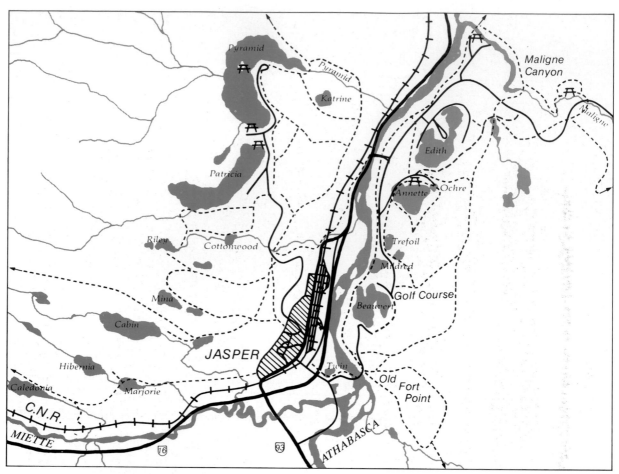

Jasper and area.

Highway 16, where the road to Miette Hotsprings branches off. Although best known for its sulphur springs and swimming pool, the Miette area offers a number of other activities such as pony riding and hiking.

Another drive is westbound on the Yellowhead Highway via the pass into British Columbia's Mount Robson Provincial Park, where, if not covered by clouds, you can admire the highest peak of the Rocky Mountains at an altitude of 3,954 metres (12,972 feet). The best view of Mount Robson is from the highway, where the Robson River streams down through Kinney Lake and via the Knowlton Falls into the Fraser River.

Provided you are in good shape, the Tonquin Valley with the Amethyst Lakes and The Ramparts to the west is a thrilling excursion both in summer and winter. During the summer you can either hike or join in on a packtrain horseback excursion through Portal Valley, passing by Marmot Mountain and Peveril Peak, and via the Maccarib Pass. You can also follow the Astoria River in its valley, where on the left side is Mount Edith Cavell and Mount Throne. Tonquin Valley is unforgettable in winter. You can go in on skis or by dog sled, overnighting

under the spectacular Ramparts in rustic backcountry cabins, where an outfitter provides supplies and other needed equipment.

Not very strenuous, but highly interesting and within unsurpassably beautiful mountain scenery, is an excursion by car to Maligne Lake about 50 km (30 miles) from Jasper. The first attraction on the Maligne Lake Road is Maligne Canyon, 50 metres (165 feet) deep, and so narrow that squirrels jump across it. The Maligne River surges through this spectacular limestone gorge before joining the Athabasca River in the valley. The canyon is a new river channel, eroded since the glaciers retreated from this region. The cold grey cliffs of the canyon seem to testify to the strength and stability of the rock; yet, at the hand of water, the rock dissolved, and cracks in the earth yawned. Mechanical abrasion by water has also worn away some of the bedrock. In the many potholes (circular depressions), suspended sediments have been captured. The rapid current will keep them circling, grinding the limestone, until the river sinks farther.

In addition to the spectacular canyon itself, hikers may observe that the volume of water in the river is much greater near Fifth Bridge than at the head of the canyon. This is caused by the

58

Jasper's Connaught
Drive with hotels,
shops, and the
Information Centre,
opposite of which is
the CN railway station.

The Jasper Park Lodge,
elegant hotel complex
at Lac Beauvert.

Summer hiking in Tonquin Valley, with the Amethyst Lakes and The Ramparts.

emergence of water from underground passages, carried all the way from Medicine Lake some 16 km (10 miles) upstream. Several of these outlets can be seen along the lower portions of the trail.

Summer visitors assume that Medicine Lake is a normal mountain lake. But local Indians spoke of it as "Bad Medicine." Each year, in fall and winter, the water level sinks and the lake disappears, becoming a clay flat with only scattered pools of water connected by a stream. The Maligne River continues to enter its southeast end, but no surface outlet from the basin is visible at the other end. The water vanishes into the lake bottom.

It was French scientist Jean Corbel who first recognized the existence of a sinking river when he visited the area in 1956. Ten years later a group from McMaster University began studies here. Using special dyes, they accomplished the first successful tracing of water from Medicine Lake to the outlets further down the valley, visible proof of underground passages. The Maligne River is one of the largest sinking rivers in the Western Hemisphere, and one researcher suggested that the Maligne system may contain one of the largest inaccessible underground cave systems anywhere in the world. As the river will continue to enlarge its underground passages, Medicine Lake may, one day, disappear forever.

After passing Medicine Lake, the narrow road upstream widens into a marvellous highway, winding through the forested valleyground between ridges of the Queen Elizabeth Ranges to the east and the Maligne Range to the west, until you reach the northern end of Maligne Lake, the largest glacier-fed lake in the Canadian Rockies, and, as most visitors admit, the most beautiful one as well. Twenty-two km (14 miles) in length, Maligne Lake is surrounded by the towering mountain peaks of the Queen Elizabeth Ranges. Almost all of them are over 3,000 metres (10,000 feet) in altitude, such as the Leah and Samson Peaks, the Maligne Mountain on the eastern shores, Mount Charlton, Llysfran Peak and Mount Mary Vaux in the west, and Monkhead and Mount Brazeau towards the south, the latter one at 3,470 metres (11,386 feet) being the tallest of them all.

You can explore Maligne Lake by hiking on the several available trails, or by canoe, rowboat or aboard one of the several commercial tour boats. Whatever way you choose, it will be an unforgettable excursion. It is not only the mountain world around the lake's shorelines, it is also the numerous small forested islands in Maligne Lake, such as famous Spirit Island, which inspire the imagination to be right in the

Coyotes are shy and noctural, and belong to the dog family.

Mule deer with its (still) furry antlers, and its long ears and black-tipped tail.

middle of the most marvellous mountain paradise on earth.

* * *

Returning to the highway and leaving the parks in whatever direction is like waking up from a beautiful dream.

"You who love beauty may you find it; you who seek rest may it come to your arms; you who worship Nature may you kneel at her altar. With these hopes we respectfully dedicate to you 'The Visitors' Guide.'" Banff, anno 1932.

61

Mountain climbing, a challenge for the sportsman, at the steep walls of the Mount Edith Cavell massives, with Angel Glacier in the background.

The "Jasper Tramway," overlooking the wide forest-and-lakes valley, where the Miette River joins the Athabasca.

ALBERTA GOVERNMENT APPROVED ACCOMMODATION

BANFF NATIONAL PARK

Name of establishment (403)		S	D/T
BANFF AND AREA			
Alpine Motel	762–2332	$ 48	$ 48
Aspen Lodge	762–3656	65	70
Banff Motel	762–2332	48	48– 51
Banff Park Lodge	762–4433	110	125
Banff Springs Hotel	762–2211	75–130	95–150
Banffshire Inn	762–2201	45– 65	45– 75
Bighorn Motel	762–3386	44– 70	44– 70
Bow View Motor Lodge	762–2261	60– 75	60– 75
Cascade Inn	762–3311	52	52– 60
Castle Mountain Village	762–3868	38– 58	38– 58
Charlton's Cedar Court	762–4485	60	70– 82
Charlton's Evergreen Court	762–4485	65	65– 82
Douglas Fir Resort	762–5591	–	86– 98
Driftwood Motor Inn	762–3727	50– 55	50– 70
Hidden Ridge	762–3544	–	50–100
Homestead Inn	762–4471	44– 70	44– 70
Inns of Banff Park	762–4581	95	100
Irwin's Motor Inn	762–4566	36– 40	36– 46
Johnston's Canyon Resort	762–2971	34	34– 44
King Edward Hotel	762–2251	37	37– 39
Mount Royal Hotel	762–3331	73– 82	73– 82
Mountview Village	762–2400	48– 96	48– 96
Pinewoods Motel & Chalets	762–5515	80	85
Ptarmigan Inn	762–2207	70	80– 85
Red Carpet Inn	762–4184	36	36– 45
The Rimrock Inn	762–3356	85	85–140
Rundle Manor Apt. Motel	762–5544	80	80– 95
Siding 29 Lodge	762–5575	50–125	50–125
Spruce Grove Motel	762–2112	46	46– 57
Storm Mountain Lodge	762–4155	58	58
Sunshine Village	762–3383	135	200
Swiss Village Lodge	762–2256	80	85
Timberline Hotel	762–2281	95–110	120–135
Traveller's Inn	762–4401	43– 90	48– 95
Tunnel Mountain Chalets	762–4515	98	98
Voyager Inn	762–3301	46– 70	51– 75
Woodland Village Inn	762–5521	45– 70	45– 80
LAKE LOUISE AREA			
Baker Creek Bungalows	522–3761	29– 35	43– 80
Chateau Lake Louise	522–3511	75–130	95–150
Deer Lodge	522–3747	45	65– 95
The Lake Louise Inn	522–3791	48–100	48–100
Moraine Lake Lodge and Cabins	no phone	45	90
Mountaineer Motel	522–3844	55	55– 62
Paradise Lodge and Bungalows	522–3595	40	40– 58
Post Hotel & Pipestone Lodge	522–3989	33– 63	33– 63

Name of establishment (403)		S	D/T
ICEFIELDS PARKWAY			
Num-Ti-Jah Lodge	no phone	45– 48	54
Parkway Lodge	no phone	55	65
(both to be reached via Red Deer Mobile Operator)			

JASPER NATIONAL PARK

Name of establishment (403)		S	D/T
ICEFIELDS PARKWAY			
Columbia Icefield Chalet	via 762–2241	35– 45	35– 45
Sunwapta Falls Bungalows	via 852–3311	24– 49	24– 49
JASPER AND AREA			
Alpine Village	852–3285	50– 65	50– 80
Andrew Motor Lodge.	852–3394	61– 63	61– 63
Astoria Motor Inn	852–3351	37– 44	37– 44
Athabasca Hotel	852–3386	35– 39	39– 43
Becker's Roaring River Chalets	852–3779	54–100	54–100
Chateau Jasper	852–5644	95	95
Diamond Motel	852–3143	55	55
Jasper House Bungalows	852–4535	50– 75	50– 75
Jasper Inn Motor Lodge	852–4461	56– 80	64– 88
Jasper Park Lodge	852–3301	192	221
Lobstick Lodge	852–4431	45	55
Marmot Motor Lodge	852–4471	46	52– 60
Mount Robson Motor Inn	852–3327	55– 59	55– 59
Patricia Lake Bungalows	852–3560	32	50
Pine Bungalows	852–3491	50	50
Pyramid Lake Bungalows	852–3536	40– 60	40– 62
Roche Bonhomme Bungalows	852–3209	48– 70	48– 70
Sawridge Hotel Jasper	852–5111	opens	soon
Tekarra Resort	852–3058	35	35– 60
Tonquin Motor Inn	852–4987	53	63
Whistler's Motor Hotel	852–3361	39– 54	46– 54
MIETTE JUNCTION & HOT SPRINGS			
Pocahontas Bungalows	866–3732	32– 55	32– 55
Miette Hot Springs Resort Motel	866–3750	45– 65	45– 65

Rate Fluctuations: The rates contained herein are given as a guideline only and are subject to change. Rates and the establishment's deposit and refund policy should be confirmed prior to making a firm reservation. Motel/hotel reservations are normally honored to 6 p.m.